Conquer The World!

How To Be Successful In Life by
Overcoming Your Fears, Phobias,
Addictions, Depression, and Anxieties
Using Cognitive Behavioral Therapy

By Crystal Johnson

Table of Contents

"The trouble with most therapy is that it helps you to feel better. But you don't get better. You have to back it up with action, action, action."

Therapist Albert Ellis (1913-2007)

PROLOGUE: THE BEGINNING OF A NEW YOU

My Story

Depression, anxiety, and abuse in various forms have raged through my family for decades. When I was growing up, my mother was an emotionally abusive alcoholic who left me largely in charge of raising my three younger siblings and enduring the constant stream of unconstructive criticism from my good-for-nothing older brother.

My father wasn't in the picture much. He only came around when Mom called him up to complain that their oldest son was being impossible. That's how she always phrased it, "Being impossible." Being impossible meant that he wouldn't stop screaming about how we were all going to hell, and it was making her and my younger siblings hysterical. Dad would come over and add his voice to the screaming until everything finally went quiet.

During these times, I retreated into myself, to the quiet little world I'd created in order to escape from my life. I always pictured something like the secluded little Chateau Chillon in Switzerland, surrounded by the placid pool of Lake Geneva on one side and the soaring mountain ranges of the Swiss Riviera on the other. I imagined myself standing in the middle of the highest turret with the clean Swiss wind in my face, smelling earth and sunshine, alone and perfectly at peace.

When my family members were hysterical and shouting and ripping each other apart, I was in my Chateau. The moment the screaming finally stopped was the moment the fictional wind left my face, and I returned to the trailer house in Missouri where I had grown up, and I picked up the remnants of the battle.

Dad would storm out, Niko would disappear into his bedroom and blast his creepy cult rap, and Mom would lock herself in the bathroom with the tub running. Lily and Vi would stare out the window, wondering when Dad would come back.

Dillon would tell me that she hated me most of all and that I was definitely going to hell, because this was all my fault. She was Niko's favorite and believed everything he said. The older she got, the more cutting her insults became and the more I retreated into myself to cope. Nothing I said had any effect on her, and, according to her, I made everything worse by existing.

A small, rational part of me knew that she was telling lies, but I was so enmeshed in my toxic family culture, that the biggest part of me agreed with her. I was useless and a waste of air and money. Everything I did failed. Everything I said was false. No one loved me. I was worthless.

Some days I was so sunk in depression that I couldn't even find my chateau, instead seeing only darkness around me and feeling nothing. Feeling nothing scared me, so I started hurting myself in order to feel something. I plucked out hairs on my legs and arms. I dug my nails into my arms until I bled. I got into the habit of knocking on my thigh with my leg just above my knee when I was alone, watching after day as the bruise blossomed, grew, shrunk, and grew again.

I spent the first twenty-five years of my life living from one crisis to the next, not understanding that life wasn't like this for everyone. It was my responsibility to go grocery shopping, my responsibility to do the laundry for the kids, and it was my responsibility to make sure the kids did their homework and stayed out of trouble in school. No one looked out for me, and I assumed that was because I didn't deserve it. Whenever the kids went to Mom with a dispute or a request, she yelled at me for failing them and bothering her with things that didn't matter.

The only person Mom never held me responsible for was my older brother. Niko did was he wanted, and I guess, even in her messed

8

up state, she understood that, unlike the younger kids, I hadn't been the one to raise him. That failure was entirely on her.

The defining moment of change came the night before my twenty-fifth birthday when Dillon had screamed at me that it was my fault she didn't have a dress for the prom, because I wouldn't give her the money. I didn't have the money because every paycheck I earned went toward keeping the household minimally functional. I told her this.

"If you weren't so stupid you could get a better job," she said. "We'd be better off without you."

Niko emerged from his room, glaring at me.

I left the house, needing to get away from them as quickly as possible, and I kept on walking.

Somewhere deep inside my brain, I knew that if she wanted a prom dress, then she should have gotten a job herself. She should have seen that I was doing the best I could for everyone with my crappy factory job that I'd been forced to take because there was never any money for me to get an education to do something better. She should have treated me with respect.

But the part of me that was too immersed in the family culture to see the irrationality of the arguments was at the helm. It was my fault. Nothing I did was good enough. I wasn't smart enough or hardworking enough or diligent enough. They really would be better off without me. Maybe it would be better if I disappeared. Maybe it would be better if I died.

I walked faster, pressing my fingernails into my palms until I felt the pinch of pain.

All of a sudden, lights sprang in front of me, and I ducked, realizing as my fingers brushed the tar that I was in the middle of the road. Brakes squealed and less than a second later, something slammed into my side. Right before I blacked out, I remember thinking, "I didn't mean to die."

I woke up in the hospital bleary-eyed and completely disoriented. Lily, my youngest sister, slept in a chair next to me. When I stirred, she bolted upright.

"You're awake," she said. "Can you come home now?" Her eyes filled with desperation.

I tried to sit, but I felt too heavy to move. Looking down I saw only my own still form under the white sheet. Was I paralyzed? I couldn't be paralyzed. "How long have I been here?" I asked. My voice felt raspy in my dry throat.

Lily shrugged. "A couple of days. I need you to take me to the store tonight. We're out of food, and Dillon said she'd pound me if I come home without any."

Dillon was going to pound on Lily because I couldn't drive her to the store, and all because I wasn't watching where I was walking in the dark.

My eyelids felt heavy, and before I could think of anything to say to Lily, I felt sleep pulling me under again.

When I next awoke, I saw a middle aged woman I'd never seen before pacing my room. She immediately went to my side as soon as my eyes opened. "You're awake," she said. "I'm so sorry about what happened to you. My lawyer said I shouldn't be here, but I needed to make sure you were okay."

I was confused. Why did it matter to her if I was okay? She didn't know me. What did she want from me?

"I swear I didn't see you in the road. I didn't see you there until it was too late, and if you want to sue me, I totally understand. I'm just so glad you're alive." She started crying.

I stared at her until she got a grip on herself. She sat down next to me, taking my hand, and something about the gesture made my own eyes well up with tears. I'd never had another person show me any compassion simply because I was another human being. I'd never believed I deserved any, and Lucy, the woman who had ironically almost killed me was the person who showed me how not okay everything in my life was.

Over the next few weeks, I underwent a painful physical recovery, and Lucy was there every step of the way. I wasn't paralyzed, but many of the nerves in my legs and shoulder had been pinched, and two bones in my left arm had been broken, so I had to relearn a lot of daily tasks like sitting up, feeding myself, and walking.

My family members visited me in the hospital on occasion, but only when they wanted me to do something or fix something for them. My mother even visited once to inform me that I needed to sue the lady who hit me for all she was worth, because I didn't give her a good enough allowance with my crummy job.

I let this eat me up for a while, but finally being away from the toxicity of my family had given me a new perspective. I didn't want to sue Lucy. She was the only one who cared enough to visit me every day and encourage me through my exercises. Maybe as Niko, and then Dillon, told me, I was being selfish, but for the first time in my life, I began to see that I could make choices.

After years of living under the influence of crippling self-doubt and the feeling that I must have deserved every bad thing that ever happened to me, I decided to change the one person, who at the end of the day, I could claim any power over: myself.

The rest of this book is all about how I reclaimed my health and life and how you can too!

What Is Cognitive Behavioral Therapy?

Cognitive behavioral therapy (CBT) is a kind of psychotherapy that integrates two popular therapeutic systems: cognitive therapy and behavioral therapy. Cognitive therapy, simply put, is a method of changing self-defeating thinking, and behavioral therapy is applying learning techniques to changing self-defeating behaviors. Cognitive therapists and researchers believe in the healing power of self-awareness, and behavioral therapists and researchers tend to assume that the behavior *is* the problem

Combining the two therapies, CBT attempts to alter behaviors and negative thought patterns about the self and the world in order to bring about healthier, more balanced views of the self and the world. CBT isn't one method of overcoming fear, anxiety, and depression so much as it is a series of many different techniques that work at varying levels for different people.

While cognitive therapies and behavioral therapies focus solely on either thoughts or behaviors, CBT is designed to be both rational and practical. You can learn to understand your thought patterns and come up with practical ways to implement change in your thoughts and in your behaviors simultaneously. Like the quote by Albert Ellis at the very beginning of this book, getting better is about far more than *feeling* better. You have to be able to support your good feelings with healthy behaviors and vice versa.

CBT consists largely of different techniques for positive self-thought that, in turn, affect behavior, but it's a lot more complex than that, as the human mind is still a bit of an unknown frontier. While I will be focusing largely on overcoming abuse, anxiety, fears, phobias, and depression, the techniques of CBT can also be used if you don't regularly experience any of those things and simply want to improve an area of your life and become a more positive, healthy person.

It's important for me to note that while CBT can be heartily effective on its own for treating mild to moderate cases of depression, anxiety, etc., more severe cases may require medication or further treatment. In severe cases, positive self-thought can be somewhat helpful, but it may be impossible to fix yourself solely through CBT. This is not your fault. Especially in the case of serious mental illness, it's not always a matter of willpower, and you shouldn't blame yourself if you're not able to completely recover from your illness without help from medicine or additional therapy.

What Is the Purpose of This Book?

This book is not meant to take the place of advice from a trained professional. While I've done personal and academic research on overcoming fears, phobias, addiction, depression, and anxiety, I am not a doctor or a therapist, and you shouldn't place my advice above that of a medical professional.

I do, however, have intimate knowledge of several techniques from CBT that can be used to overcome depression, anxiety, fear, and addiction that I intend to share with you. With these techniques, I will also provide a background of how each condition being treated is defined, as there are many misconceptions about what it means to live with some of these problems.

By the end of this book, my goal is that you would have some practical techniques to help you overcome the things about yourself that hinder your ability to live your life to the fullest. While I will be addressing this book to you, the reader, I know that you may be reading this book in order to understand and help a friend or loved one rather than yourself. I applaud you, and I sincerely hope that this little book can give you some insight and helpful techniques.

Finally, I want to leave you empowered with the reminder that got me through many long days of recovery after my accident: you are a human being worthy of respect and full of dignity. It's time for you to conquer those things in your life that make you feel like less than yourself.

CHAPTER ONE: AN OVERVIEW OF COGNITIVE BEHAVIORAL THERAPY STEPS AND TECHNIQUES

Cognitive Behavioral Therapy is used to treat and cope with many physical and emotional challenges, including anxiety, depression, fear, addiction, eating disorders, grief, distressing life situations, PTSD, and a variety of other challenges for which thought patterns can play a pivotal role.

The premise of CBT is to help you identify areas of your life in which your own thought patterns and behaviors are undermining your ability to meet your needs or goals. Then, CBT seeks to undo the negative thought patterns by learning new patterns to replace the old ones. If you were to go to a therapist for CBT, this process of relearning healthy thoughts, you should expect that it should take anywhere from ten to twenty sessions over the course of two to four months. While it's considered to be a short-term therapy, results aren't always immediate and easy to obtain.

This chapter is meant to give you an overview of what CBT is and how it works before we jump into talking about its usage in specific areas of your life.

What is the Process of Cognitive Behavioral Therapy?

CBT consists broadly of a list of steps that are used to overcome negative thought or behavior patterns. These steps are the bedrock of CBT, and once you understand them, you will be equipped to overcome those areas of your life from which your own thoughts are holding you back from success.

Identify Your Life's Problematic Situations or Conditions

It can be hard to honestly examine your own life and see the abnormalities and areas of trouble, but this step is imperative to the process of recovery. The goal here is to find the thing or things that will help you uncover the roots of your problems. This means that you have to be honest with yourself and admit that there is a problem. Don't let your shame or guilt get in the way of your recovery. The real shame is in ignoring or denying your problems.

These situations or conditions might be a death in the family, a recent divorce, symptoms of a mental illness, an ongoing physical sickness, financial strain, an abusive relationship, or any of a number of things that feed into your worldview and how you feel about yourself and others.

For me, it was hard to see the extent of my problems right away when I was so close to my family, and some of the situations and conditions I lived through became apparent to me only gradually. All you can do is start with what you know to be a problem. I started by acknowledging the constant strain of having Niko and Dillon belittle me. I came to realize that my parents' absence as parents and the fact that I was raising my little sisters essentially alone were also conditions under which I lived, and I finally was able to acknowledge my depression as a huge problem that I needed to overcome.

Become Aware of Thoughts, Feelings, and Beliefs About Problems

Once you've identified the problematic situations in your life, the next step in the CBT process is to make yourself aware of what these situations make you think and feel about yourself and others. The manner in which you think about things shapes your thoughts and therefore your feelings and beliefs about yourself and others.

When my therapist asked me to tell her about my depression, I described it as the room of blackness and nothingness inside my head where I went when I didn't deserve to go to my chateau. I said that I was afraid of it and tried to ward it off with pain to my body. I thought that I was worthless and believed that I didn't deserve love or anything good. Somehow, this life I got was the life I deserved, and it was proof of my inadequacy that I couldn't seem to overcome it.

My therapist was able to highlight for me the negative thoughts and beliefs that fed my depression and led me on a downward spiral. If you don't have a therapist, or even if you do, starting a journal of your thoughts and feelings can be a helpful, concrete way of becoming more self-aware and a step closer to overcoming your problems.

Identify Negative, Inaccurate Thinking

Once you've identified what your thoughts or feelings are about a particular situation, it's time to get to the meat of CBT and identify for yourself where your negative or inaccurate thought patterns are.

Inaccurate thought patterns are assumptions that you make about yourself and others that don't reflect reality as it is objectively. Often, these are thoughts that you repeat to yourself, perhaps subconsciously, until they become beliefs that negatively transform the way you experience life. Because these thoughts are slippery and often subconscious, it can be hard to see your harmful thought patterns on your own. This is another reason why it's helpful to keep a journal. You might also find an insightful confidant who is good about being honest with you, like a therapist.

For me, I felt that I deserved to be unhappy because it was my own fault that my life was so messed up. My therapist was able to point out to me that I often used the word "deserve" to describe my life situation. I thought in terms of things that I did and didn't deserve. Once I realized that this was a common thread in my thoughts about my family and my depression, it was like the enemy to my happiness was congealing in the air before me, and it was finally time to battle it.

Replace Negative or Inaccurate Thought Patterns

Replacing your negative views of self can be an extremely difficult uphill battle, especially when these views have been ingrained in your for years, but it's imperative to conquering your inner demons and becoming your best self. With the identified thought patterns from the previous step, you will need to ask yourself some tough questions about why you believe these inaccurate or negative thoughts and what the reality of the situation is.

Depending on what the thought pattern is that you're trying to overcome, you may need an outside perspective to help you figure out where and how reality and your perception of it diverge.

You might think of those super nanny TV shows in which an expert would come into a home and identify all the false perceptions and misconceptions of the parents that propelled bad behavior in their children.

It's valuable to have a friend or two or some kind of support group outside of the context of your situation to take a look at the problem you are experiencing and help you see where your thoughts and beliefs are wrong and what's actually going on.

As I explained pieces of my life to Lucy, she served as a sounding board. Her genuine shock at the way my siblings and mother treated me gave me hope that some of my problems could be overcome simply by being made aware of how my situation fueled untrue beliefs about myself and changing the thoughts inside of my head.

Instead of constantly telling myself that I deserved to suffer and that everything was my fault, I gradually learned to assign the blame where it was due and take only that which I truly had any control over. In fact, for a while, I found that it was best for me to eliminate "deserve" from my vocabulary, because it triggered in me what too easily became a downward spiral of self-blame.

I reminded myself that I wasn't my siblings' mother, and she was the one who was supposed to be responsible for them. I repeated positive thoughts to myself over and over in order to ingrain them in my mind and get them to replace the bitter, self-loathing thoughts that had accompanied me for twenty-five years.

Recondition Your Behaviors

While cognitive therapy would stop with reconditioning thoughts, CBT seeks to reinforce alternative thought patterns with positive behaviors that run contrary to the negative thoughts. For example, when things became dark and unbearable for me at home, and I felt the urge to pluck my hair or make myself bleed, I instead made myself say that I was worthy of respect and dignity and then go reinforce my positive statement by going for a run or visiting the library—things I discovered that I like to do.

The positive activity doesn't have to be anything too complex. You could read a magazine article, garden, take a walk, play with your dog, or any number of things that you normally like to do.

Hang In There

Finally, once you've started attacking negative thoughts with positive ones, reshaping your worldview into something healthier, and reinforcing your positive thinking with positive activities, the key is to hang in there. It's not always going to be easy to believe in your new positive thinking techniques, especially if you are not able to remove yourself from the problematic situation, but keep heart. The amazing plasticity of the human brain means that with practice and time, the new positive thought pattern you are trying to learn will become a habit and eventually take less mental effort to sustain.

One technique that can help you to hang in there is to, at the end of the day, visualize the most positive parts of your day. This activity is meant to keep you from wallowing in the things that didn't go as well as you wished them to and to force you to acknowledge what you did well.

Another thing that will help you hang in there is learning to accept disappointment as a normal part of life without drowning in it. Feeling sad and disappointed about things is a natural part of human existence, and denying your legitimate feelings about something bad going on in your life is not healthy or helpful to your long-term mental health. Instead, allow yourself to feel the emotion but instead of blaming yourself or falling back on your old habits, remind yourself that even though you feel sad or angry, you are still worthy of respect and dignity.

CBT won't prevent you from ever feeling unhappy or downtrodden, but it can help you to find healthy ways to manage sadness and disappointment without reverting back to inaccurate negative thoughts that feed your anxiety, fear, or depression and put you back at square one.

Common Patterns of Negative Self-Thought

Aaron T. Beck, commonly believed to be the father of modern cognitive therapy, believed that many dysfunctional thought patterns are often formed in childhood but can be fixed through a process called cognitive restructuring, which, simply put, means replacing negative self-talk with positive self-talk.

Identifying and changing patterns of negative self-thought can sound straightforward enough until you actually try doing it yourself. The following are some patterns that will help you identify and label potentially harmful patterns within your own thoughts and some pointers for going to battle against them.

All Or Nothing Thinking

You ate that piece of cake instead of reaching for the fruit; you must be a bad person. You smoked that cigarette instead of sticking with your strict cold-turkey regimen; you must be a complete failure. You accidentally lost your cool and yelled at your child to obey you, and it backfired; you must be a terrible parent. You couldn't confront your fear of crowds and backed out of a social function at the last moment; you must be a horrible friend.

All of these are examples of all or nothing thinking. You tell yourself that if you failed at one thing, then you must therefore be failing at all of it. This is a lie. The truth is that any step forward you take is a success, and any failure on your part is only that: one failure that is not indicative of your entire self-worth.

You are far better than one mistake or one relapse. A mistake is not a failure, because you are not giving up.

Over-Personalizing

You blame yourself for your contentious family. You blame yourself for being overweight. You blame yourself for not being able to pull yourself out of you depression by sheer willpower. You blame yourself for getting cancer, because you should have been more careful about your diet or more diligent with your doctor visits.

This is called over-personalizing, in which you grant yourself the blame for things that are outside of your control. I was very guilty of this, and the thought pattern threatened to derail many of my strides forward with its recurring accusations.

Some things are simply not your fault, and it's completely useless for you to take credit for them. I took credit for my siblings' poor behavior, when it was my parents' parenting style that should have taken the credit. Lucy told said to me one day, "Don't you think it's awfully egotistical of you to take all of the blame for your family's troubles? It's not all about you. Much of it is on them, and there's nothing you could have done to change it." The statement was, admittedly, a little insensitive, but it shocked me into agreement. Of course there were things beyond my control, and to believe that I should be able to control them was like saying I thought I was God or something.

If a situation is genuinely your fault, then take credit, but only take the amount of credit that is yours to take. Be honest with yourself either way. I know better than most that for some of us, it's harder to reject the blame than it is to accept all of it.

Catastrophic Thinking

You can't find the energy to go to work today, so you must be a failure at life. You couldn't overcome your social anxiety to meet with a colleague today, so you must suck at your job. You ate a doughnut from the box someone brought the office this afternoon instead of exercising, so you must be fat and lazy and sloppy.

These are catastrophic thought patterns. They are categorized by immediately jumping to the most extreme conclusion possible. You place an exaggerated importance on each seeming failure or blip in your happiness.

When you find yourself stuck in catastrophic thinking, it's helpful to have someone positive in your life to remind you of the faulty logic of catastrophic thinking, that one failure doesn't equal a failed you. If you find yourself immediately jumping to the worst conclusion about yourself, take a breath and remind yourself that you are a good person worthy of happiness and success and that one mistake doesn't seal your identity as bad or unworthy.

Getting the Most Out Of CBT

CBT requires consistent effort from you if you want to get the best results possible from it. Whether you are seeing a therapist or working through your problems on your own, there are a variety of things you should make sure not to slack on if you want to conquer your own mind.

Be Honest

Whether your seeing a therapist, talking with a friend, or writing to yourself in your journal, it's important that you are one hundred percent honest with yourself and those trying to help you. It will be tempting to shy away from difficult emotions, but if you want CBT to help you succeed, that is not an option.

I didn't want to tell people about the pain I inflicted on myself in my lowest moments, because I was embarrassed, ashamed, and afraid of judgment, but when I ignored this aspect of my life, somehow it validated the self-harm, and I did it all the more. Once I told Lucy how much I wanted to hurt myself some days, I was able to confront another symptom of my depression and work toward treating it.

If you're not honest about as much as possible, you risk losing everything you've worked for, like an undercover scandal can ruin an entire election for a political candidate. You're not running for office; you're running for you. Be honest.

Stick With the Plan

You won't always feel like doing the things you should—going to your therapy sessions, meeting that supportive friend for coffee, showing up to the fun activity that you scheduled for yourself, following through on the next stage of facing your fear—and at those times it will be tempting to say, "Screw it. I'll deal with it tomorrow." But falling off the wagon one time will make it that much harder to get back up on the wagon and stay there for the next phase of your treatment.

As in the case of depression, you might feel like you have no control and like you physically can't get out of bed or summon the energy to do what you know you should. If at all possible, set up a support network to help you in those times. Lucy was the person who motivated me. I'd call her and tell her I wasn't going to make it to coffee with her, and she came to my house and made me leave the chores behind, even if Mom was screaming and Dillon was swearing at me. I didn't appreciate it at the time, because treating myself felt like an unnecessary and undeserved privilege, but she helped me keep the momentum of my treatment going.

Find Additional Improvement Opportunities

Sometimes this simply means doing whatever homework your therapist assigns you between sessions. Maybe this is journaling, repeating positive statements to yourself daily, or reading a book or an article.

You can also come up with things on your own to supplement your improvement. Maybe you decide to treat yourself to reading a chapter of a book you like every day. Maybe that's treating yourself to a spa day on occasion. Maybe that's simply taking a few moments to focus on a beautiful tree or an interesting thing that you learned or saw that day.

Be Realistic

You might experience instant results, but you probably won't. Healing and recovery take time, and you need to be fair to yourself and allow yourself to take the time you need. A lot of CBT treatments are meant as short-term treatments, but, depending on the issue you intend to overcome, it could take a lot longer to fully eliminate harmful thinking from your repertoire and replace it with the kind of thoughts that let you conquer the world.

If you're overcoming drug addiction, you might still struggle with an unhealthy desire to take drugs in extreme situations. CBT gives you the tools you need to cope with the struggle, but it doesn't always take away the struggle.

Sometimes, while CBT can help you cope with a problem, it can't solve the problem for you. For example I haven't been able to make my mother stop drinking and badmouthing me to my siblings, but CBT has helped me cope with my own thoughts and feelings that result from my mother's actions and words. Another example is a chronic physical illness. CBT can help you make the most of your life while living with diabetes or cancer, but it's unlikely to cure your disease.

Understanding that both you and CBT have limitations will help you make the most of yourself and of the treatment.

CHAPTER TWO: OVERCOMING ABUSE AND TRAUMATIC STRESS

Sometimes anxious thought patterns, fears, depression, and addictions are, at least in part, the result of abuse or traumatic stress, which is why I'm starting with a chapter about using CBT to overcome these abusive or traumatic experiences.

People deal with abuse and stress in different ways, and while some bounce back quickly and seemingly unscathed and without repercussions, others get caught in dangerous cycles of denial, blame, self-loathing, depression, anxiety, obsessive compulsive tendencies, and any number of other harmful behaviors and thought patterns that are not conducive to happiness or good health.

The truth is that you might not have the power to stop or leave the abusive situation, but you do have the power to learn how to think about the abuse and its repercussions in a healthy manner and then choose how to respond. That is what this chapter will be about.

Abuse can range from the physical, violent, or sexual, to the subtle and emotional. Abuse doesn't always look the same in every circumstance, and its effects vary so much from one person to the next that it makes it an extremely difficult subject to address, especially since perceptions of abuse vary widely from one culture, and even one household to another. Words that constitute a fun time for all in one family might be a toxic mess of verbal abuse in another.

Likewise, when you're in an abusive situation, it's easy to write off the situation as normal and assume that the problem isn't with the situation but with you. This is called emotionally abusive self-talk, which I will also talk about in this chapter.

Defining Abuse and Trauma

Abuse is defined as repeated cruelty or violence to a person or animal. More precisely, it is words or behaviors designed to subjugate a person through fear, coercion, manipulation, guilt, humiliation, intimidation, or violence. People commonly think of abuse as only being physical or sexual crimes against another person's body and discount other kinds of abuse as less severe or less important. However, anytime someone is manipulating your actions or emotions in such a way that you start to disbelieve your own perceptions and emotions, it's abuse.

In the case of emotional abuse, the victim often feels fearful, isolated from other members of society, and diminished in self-esteem and self-worth. Because emotional abuse is not always blatant, it can be slippery to pinpoint and easy to explain away.

He's criticizing me because he had a bad day. He's telling me I'm stupid because people at his job are telling him he's stupid. He's just telling me things about myself that are true. He's just being honest with me. He's talking over my arguments and not listening to me because I'm making irrational points, and I don't make any sense. The justifications for emotional abuse run the gamut from the seemingly sensible to the completely irrational.

Trauma can result from abuse, but more broadly defined, it's usually an emotional response to a deeply distressing occurrence, like a car accident, the death of a loved one, rape, assault, war, or any number of events that can result in emotional disturbance. According to the American Psychological Association, shock and denial are typical immediate reactions to trauma, and common long-term effects include flashbacks, unpredictable emotions, strain in relationships, and sometimes even physical symptoms.

Like with abuse, trauma also can skew your perception of self and hinder the manner in which you speak to yourself.

Common Thought Patterns that Result from Long-Term Abuse

Victims of abuse often have a difficult time differentiating between the truth and the skewed reality of their abuser. And abuser might say or insinuate that you don't deserve good things, that you are worthless, that you asked for it, that your opinion is stupid, that you don't matter, and that it's your fault.

Hearing negative statements like that over and over wires your brain to expect them, and, over time, to start regurgitating them subconsciously. Even if consciously you don't believe that you're stupid, hearing the words repeated by a bully or an abuser can train your mind to recall those words most quickly in other situations.

Basic learning principles tell us that we become what we practice. The more we practice, the more ingrained the neural pathways become. When we practice saying, "You're stupid," or, "You don't deserve to eat," over time, these become the words that we use to talk to ourselves.

In an abusive situation you're practicing negative thought patterns through reinforcement from your abuser, and eventually you learn to emotionally abuse yourself through emotionally abusive self-talk.

Self-talk and your behavioral choices are what the remainder of this chapter is about.

CBT Techniques for Dealing with Emotionally Abusive Self-Talk

There are a variety of techniques that you can use to become more aware of your thought patterns, how they affect you, and what you can do to improve the landscape of your thoughts.

Mindfulness

Imagine seeing your thoughts like leaves in a flowing river or boxes on a conveyor belt. Close your eyes and notice some of the things that you tell yourself. What is your mind saying about you? Don't judge yourself. Are you thinking about your to-do list? Are you thinking about your brother criticizing you for not having his laundry done when he told you to do it? Are you thinking about how stupid you felt when you mother asked why you couldn't just do what you were told? Are you thinking about a presentation you're supposed to give at work tomorrow?

As you let your thoughts flow over you, take note of the emotions that come with the thoughts. Are you thinking about a situation? What are you telling yourself about the situation? Are you telling yourself that if you fail your exam then it's proof that your boyfriend is right and you had no business trying to waste money on going back to school?

Notice, too, how often your mind goes to certain thoughts.

Mindfulness meditation can be a great way to help you deepen your understanding of what kinds of things you tell yourself.

Shift Perspectives

Once you're aware of your thoughts and emotions, pick one. Maybe you're thinking about your test and your boyfriend telling you that you wasted money on something selfish. You're stupid and can't do this. Those are the thought in your head. Now ask yourself what are five other possible perspectives. Maybe you have studied and worked hard, and you've learned a lot from this class regardless of whether you fail. Maybe your boyfriend is being unfair and mean to you.

Shifting perspectives allows you to step back from your point of view and become a little more objective. It allows you the opportunity to reframe an issue. Are you stupid and likely to fail? Or are you working hard letting your abuser's words get inside of your head and become your own?

Accept Reality

This is as much about letting yourself acknowledge that you feel certain emotions about being abused—shame, guilt, anger—as it is about not making reality even worse by perpetuating the words of your abuser within your own mind.

Remember that not all feelings are in your head. Emotional responses are the body's natural alarm system. Guilt is a signal that maybe I've made a mistake. So I ask myself if I've made a mistake. If I have, then I figure out how to fix it, learn from it, and move on. If I haven't made a mistake, then I set the emotion aside and move on. Don't get stuck on justifying your thought or emotion when you're already determined that it's not based in fact.

Accepting reality means that you don't ignore thoughts and feelings, but you also don't give them undue importance. Remember that acceptance and approval are not the same thing. You can accept a situation without endorsing it.

When you accept reality, you are open to make some choices. "This is what my situation is. I can either do X, Y, or Z." In my situation, once I stopped minimizing and discrediting myself and worked to see my situation clearly, it was still hard and overwhelming. I was still tempting to hurt myself or run. The difference was that I could consciously lay out choices for myself. Ignore Niko. Walk outside. Take deep breaths. Tell myself three positive things about myself. I am strong. I can do this. I deserve respect.

Regulate Emotions

Emotional regulation is the ability to use emotions as a resource instead of being controlled by them. Emotions are information, not fact. In the case of abuse, your anger might signify that you're being mistreated. Your shame might signify that you've done something wrong. Examine the situation as objectively as possible.

If you have the thought that you're stupid, you might ask why you feel that way. Maybe it's the voice of your abuser. If that's the case, give it a nod of acknowledgement, and refocus your attention on something else.

Says Dr. LuAnn Helms, "I don't have control over who knocks at my door, but I do have control over how long I entertain them." You can't always dictate which thoughts will enter your mind, but you can make a choice about how long they will stay there.

Accountability

Accountability is different than shame. Shame is like saying, "I am a mistake," rather than, "I made a mistake."

Minimizing, denial, and blame are bad habits that get in the way of accountability. Minimizing is saying that a problem isn't as bad as it is. Denial is pretending the problem doesn't exist. Blame is skirting the problem by taking on all of the responsibility or none of it. These are especially common for abuse victims.

For a long time, my instinct was to minimize my situation and accept all of the blame or to simply withdraw into my own world and pretend that it didn't exist. With accountability, you can't do any of those things. Accountability is all about accepting the problem for what it is and focusing on what you will choose to do about it.

Positive Self-Talk

Every time your abuser or your abuser's voice in your head tells you something bad about yourself, tell yourself something positive. Maybe say the opposite. When you hear, "You're a selfish, uncaring person," tell yourself, "I am empathetic and caring." Repeat the positive words several times. There's a good chance you won't believe yourself, especially at first. However, the reinforcement of positive thinking will give your brain a greater breadth of cognitive complexity in future situations.

Behavioral therapists believe that learning the right behavior and practicing it can lead to the right thoughts. The same principle applies with positive self-talk. Even if you don't believe that you are awesome and worthy, tell yourself anyway. Then treat yourself as if you believe the good things you are telling yourself. Over time, your true thoughts will fall in line with your behavior.

When you catch yourself repeating a negative thought to yourself that came from your abuser, it can help to step back and ask yourself, "Would I talk to my friend in the same way I talk to myself?" Would you repeat to your friend that they are stupid, ugly, or worthless? No, you would not. So don't tell yourself that garbage.

Finally, you become what you practice, so practice focusing on the good parts of your day or the moments when you felt good about yourself. As you're falling asleep at night, instead of worrying about the handful of things that happened outside of your control that made you feel terrible, think about that moment when you caught a glimpse of the beautiful sunset or about how peaceful it was to be awake early in the morning, long before anyone has awoken, or about the happiness that filled you when you pet the soft kitten from the neighbor's house.

The Trauma Model of Overcoming Abuse Through CBT

According to an article in *Social Work Today* by Lindsey Getz, it's common for abuse, especially child sexual abuse, to be swept under the proverbial rug and ignored. Nobody likes to talk about such issues or hear about them, and those who experience them consequently go unheard and are left to suffer in silence. CBT states, however, that silence is the opposite of how we should respond. Studies have shown instead that a key part of overcoming trauma and abuse is being able to walk through it, acknowledge it, and correct any assumptions that may have formed as a result.

Some people believe that talking about a traumatic event or an abusive situation is in itself traumatic, which further perpetuates silence on the issue. However, the evidence doesn't support avoidance as an effective method of dealing with abuse and trauma. You don't overcome a fear of heights by avoiding heights. You don't overcome fear and anxiety from abuse by avoiding any discussion about abuse. Since it's hard to talk about abuse, especially at first, it's often best to ease into it. Start small, and gradually fill in the details.

Over time, you will be able to work your way through the CBT techniques for overcoming abuse listed previously.

When Is CBT Inappropriate In Dealing With Abuse and Trauma?

When the trauma took place in infancy before conscious memory of the trauma could have been formed, then CBT can still have some level of effectiveness, but not to the same degree as someone with memory of the abuse they experienced.

If you are actively suicidal, you should seek assistance immediately. Thoughts of suicide are dangerous, and if you're having them, you need to stabilize yourself before trying to learn CBT techniques.

CHAPTER THREE: OVERCOMING FEARS AND PHOBIAS

We all fear something. Fear is a natural part of life developed in the early stages of evolution to help us live longer and protect us from the things that could kill us. Things like a fear of heights, fear of snakes or other wild animals, fear of social ostracizing, and fear of starvation are primal and have protected the human species for thousands of years. A certain amount of fear is good and healthy. Fear can even be a powerful motivator for meeting work deadlines and for social justice causes.

This chapter will focus on the other kind of fear—the fear that, rather than protecting us, debilitates us and keeps us from meeting our own basic needs and accomplishing our goals. This chapter will focus on the bad kind of fear and give you some practical techniques to overcome it.

What is the Difference Between Fear and Phobia?

The words fear and phobia are often used interchangeably. Fear is a natural response to an thing, event, or place that we find to be frightening. You might feel dizzy while climbing a ladder because you fear heights.

A phobia is having an irrational response to a fear, perhaps altering your lifestyle in order to avoid a thing, event, or place at all costs. If you fear dogs, you might find your heart racing when you encounter one. If you have a phobia of dogs, you might obsessively worry over encountering a dog, even when there are none present. You might go out of your way to avoid places where you might conceivably encounter a dog. You might limit your pool of friends to include only non dog owners. In other words, your fear of dogs is dictating the manner in which you live you live to an unhealthy extreme.

In a recent study of 130 dental patients with a dental phobia, the patients were asked to complete six to ten sessions of CBT. Of these patients, 103 were able to have dental work done without sedation after an average of five CBT sessions (Heidari, et. al. 2015). Because phobias are often complicated by other mental health and anxiety problems, there will still be some who require additional treatment in order to overcome the phobia, but for 80 percent of people, CBT is an extremely effective way to deal with the fear.

This chapter will give insight into both fears and phobias and give the techniques that can be used to conquer both of them.

CBT Techniques For Overcoming Fears and Phobias

Common phobias include, fear of water, flying, heights, the dark, certain animals or bugs, enclosed spaces, blood, bodily harm, vomiting, and the dentist. Statistically between ten and twenty percent of people will develop some kind of a phobia over their lifetime. They are usually developed in childhood, but they have been known to develop at any point in a person's life.

If you have one of these phobias, or another one, you probably understand that your fear is irrational or excessive, but knowing that doesn't make you less afraid or stop your body's physiological reaction to the phobia. While CBT might not make the phobia go away completely, it does offer practical solutions for dealing with them while you are experiencing the anxiety and fear.

Identify Your Thoughts

Phobias usually are intensified through conscious or subconscious rumination and worry while anticipating the stressful situation. Often, it is this rumination that builds up your anxiety until contact with the subject of the phobia results in panic. The fight or flight response is then summoned, increasing levels of fear and panic.

Mindfulness-based CBT teaches you to become aware not only of how you think and feel about your phobia but to notice when you are caught up in harmful ruminations about it. The more you worry, the more power you give to your phobia. Instead, stop the rumination. Acknowledge your feeling of fear. It won't do you any good to deny something you are feeling. That will just be confusing and create further problems. The adrenaline rush that you are experiencing is your body's natural alarm system to alert you to fear.

Rather than denying that you fear any fear, ask yourself if you are being rational. There are situations that warrant fear. Even someone who doesn't have a phobia of dogs might experience fear if a dog is ferociously barking and running at them. If, however, your situation does not warrant the level of fear that you are feeling, then you have a few options in terms of getting a grip on your body's fear response.

Minimize Physical Symptoms

If you find that your breath is coming too quickly, you are lightheaded, and your heart rate is spiraling out of control, the easiest thing to do to gain control in this situation is to breathe deeply. Take slow, controlled breaths in through your nose and diaphragm and out through your mouth, leaving a second or two of space between each breath. Many experts believe that panic attacks are sometimes brought on by a tendency to breathe too quickly. Slowing your breath forcing a measure of control back to your body.

Calm breathing won't take away your fearful feelings, but with practice it should help you feel less out of control while you experience fearful feelings.

Even if you are not prone to panic attacks, but you need to calm yourself before walking out on stage and giving the speech you prepared in front of a thousand people, it can help you get a grip on your shakiness and nerves by standing still for a moment and take half a dozen slow, deep breaths.

Another thing you can do to minimize your physical symptoms is to remember and repeat to yourself that your symptoms are harmless. Feeling sweaty or breathless can't hurt you. Feeling dizzy won't kill you. You don't need to fear your symptoms.

Finally, the best long-term technique you can use to minimize your symptoms is to use a process of gradual exposure.

Fact or Opinion

The Fact or Opinion skill helps you differentiate between that which you subjectively fear and that which is objectively fearful. A fact will have undisputed evidence. And opinion is your personal view, which is arguable and driven by your emotions rather than your logic.

Fear responses are usually fueled by emotions, which are subjective and not always reliable. They cause you to act impulsively.

If you have a phobia of dogs, you might have a thought like, "There's a dog. It looks like it wants to bite me. Get out of here!"

When you are experiencing fear, it's good to ask yourself, "Fact, or opinion?"

There is a dog here. Fact.

The dog looks like it wants to bite me. Opinion.

Getting out of here is the only option. Opinion.

My own variation on this technique is called Fact of Fiction. This technique works well on social phobias in which rumination about yourself and your shortcomings is especially rampant.

Being around strangers makes me fearful. Fact.

I will throw up in front of them. Have you ever done this before? No? This is a fiction disguised as a fact.

They will think I'm pathetic and stupid. Fiction.

Any statements that you make to yourself that you can't prove or that aren't objectively true are fictions. We all build fictions in our minds, especially in relation to what we think others' perceptions of us are. Some of these are more probable than others, and it's important to be able to differentiate between a possibility that you are making up and a probability or a fact.

If you are terrified of talking to strangers because you fear saying the wrong things, you might say to yourself, "Last time I talked to a stranger I got tongue tied." That's a fact. You might further say to yourself, "The person I was speaking to thought I was stupid and boring."

Does the evidence support this? Perhaps this is a fiction that you created.

Being able to separate facts from fiction will go a long way toward helping you analyze what you are thinking and whether you should give in to your gut reaction of fear.

Needle and Blood Phobias

Needle and blood phobias are different from other phobias. Normally, the adrenaline response will make your heart rate quicken and your blood pressure rise. In this adrenaline rush, you won't be able to faint even if you feel light-headed. In needle and blood phobias, however, after the initial adrenaline rush, there is often a sudden extreme drop in blood pressure. This is when the fainting happens.

If you have a needle or a blood phobia, a behavioral technique that can help you is called the applied tension technique. To try this technique, sit in a chair and tense all of the muscles in your body, arms, and legs except for those in your face and head. Hold the tension for ten to fifteen seconds. You should experience warmth spreading into your head and face.

Over a period of twenty to thirty seconds, release the tension from your body, until you are once again sitting normally. Repeat this five times. The whole exercise with its repetitions should take you about five minutes.

Repeat this activity several times a day for a week to get the hang of it. You should not get a headache from this technique. If you do, it probably means that you were tensing muscles in your face or head along with the rest of your body. The muscles in your face and head should be completely relaxed.

Create Rational Responses

Often it's not the situation itself that inspires fear; it's your perception about the situation. It's the thing you tell yourself about a certain situation that color your perspective and make you fearful. Monitor your thoughts and try to see them objectively. Fear is a signal that maybe you are in danger, but you are not in danger every time you are afraid. Implement a space between your thought and your action. Acknowledge your fear, and rather than acting impulsively, take a second or a minute to consciously decide what to do about it.

Maybe being in the enclosed space makes you feel afraid and short of breath. Before you instinctively panic, pause, take some deep breaths, and give yourself a choice: do you want to let the emotion dictate what you do, or do you want to calmly walk towards the exit while breathing deeply?

Your thoughts can easily become traps. Remove the traps by providing yourself with a choice.

Additionally, learn to recognize when and how your thoughts stray from the present. If you find yourself repeatedly worrying about the future, this only fuels your fear and anxiety. The present moment usually only becomes too difficult to bear if your thoughts are straying into the past or the future.

Finally, you become what you repeatedly practice. If you lie awake at night and deliberate over that moment you felt most afraid today, then you're practicing being afraid. When you notice that you're thinking about your fear, acknowledge that the fear exists and choose to find a happy emotion to practice. When did you feel happy today? What made you excited? When did you feel the most serene?

Ultimately, your goal should be to choose behaviors that are in line with the person you would like to become. Don't discredit your fears, but you don't have to let them dictate how you live your life.

CHAPTER FOUR: OVERCOMING ADDICTIONS

I wish that I could tell you a happy story about my mother using CBT to overcome her alcohol addiction. I wish I could say that at this point she has realized the extent of the destruction her addiction has caused our family. I wish I could say that we are all happy now and on our way to thriving.

So far, none of that has happened. She drinks as much as ever—maybe more—and lives in denial that any of the problems in her household are in any way her fault. The only time I hear from her is when she's having problems with my sisters that she doesn't want to deal with.

It's been tempting to blame myself for my mother's continued addiction. After all, she does. I know of all these techniques that could help her, but they are useless to my mother because she's not ready to listen to them. CBT isn't magic. You don't have the power to wave it over a loved one with an addiction and have them magically go through the magical, transformative healing process. It's a hard thing to hear that sometimes there's nothing you can do. But it's not your fault.

In order for CBT to work, the addict has to acknowledge that he or she has a problem and decide to change. If that's you or someone you know, you've come to the right place. I'm glad to share what I know. This chapter isn't an exhaustive list of techniques, and I would advise you to find a support system, whether that's a local chapter of AA or a friend who will hold you accountable when you hit a rough patch.

Whether the addiction is alcohol, drugs, nicotine, food, shopping, or any number of other behaviors, you can beat this.

Reasons For Addictions

Addiction doesn't usually occur independently of other emotional or psychological issues, which is why CBT is often extremely effective at thwarting addictive behaviors. In many cases harmful addictions are being used as coping mechanisms for situations that are otherwise too hard or painful to deal with.

An alcohol or drug addiction might stem from depression over the loss of a child or sibling. An addiction to overeating might stem from low self-esteem triggered by your mother's constant comments about your weight or inability to find and be in a stable romantic relationship.

The following are some possible reasons behind addictions that CBT can help you deal with. Once you identify what the root of your addiction is, you can start to replace the negative trigger with something positive that will help you develop healthy behavior.

Anxiety, Depression, or Mental Illnesses

Maybe you feel a constant anxiety or that you might have a mental illness. These things are a huge burden to deal with, and maybe you feel ashamed that you don't know how to make yourself normal. Performing the addictive behavior is the one way you can think of to still make yourself feel happy or normal sometimes. If you're depressed, you may have found that taking certain drugs give you a happiness or high that you are unable to experience in your normal life. For example, cocaine can relieve depression, or help a person with attention deficit to focus (Segell, 1998).

Control

The addictive behavior may be the one aspect of your life that you feel like you have any control over, whether it's gambling, eating, shopping, internet porn, or using drugs. Maybe you feel like everything else in your life is completely hopeless or out of control, and this behavior feels like something that you can have eminence over. It might have started out as an interest that you could control and then exploded into an obsession and a need to continue with it until, ironically, the thing that you thought you had control over now controls you.

Everyone's Doing It

Perhaps you got hooked on your addictive behavior back when it seemed like that's just what you had to do in order to be cool and fit in. You might have sought the approval of a role model who also did it or liked the way people treated you when you did it. Maybe you still seek the approval of others by performing the addictive behavior.

Genetic Predisposition

Some people are more susceptible to addictive behaviors than others. If your family has a history of addiction, then certain stressors within your environment may have preyed on your predisposition to addiction. While CBT can't fix your genetics, it can help you find ways to alter your environment to minimize your need for the addiction.

Painful Past

There might be something traumatic in your past that you want to cover up, and your addiction has served as a coping mechanism to help you deal with that or cover it up. A lot of victims of abuse and sexual assault turn to drugs, alcohol, eating disorders, or other addictive behaviors or substances in order to mask the overwhelming emotions of the past. It might have been the best way to cope that you could think of when you started the addictive behavior. Maybe you experienced parental rejection as a child, and turned to food as a replacement for parental love and attention.

These reasons are not exhaustive by any stretch of the imagination, but hopefully they help you to see that addiction is a lot more complex than just doing something bad over and over and hoping that somehow everything turns out well in the end. An addiction is way more complex and deeply rooted than a habit like stuttering when you get nervous or drinking a protein shake every morning for breakfast.

The Psychology of Addiction

Addiction is more than a mere habit. If you want to break a habit you can choose to apply some willpower and break it with no real psychological repercussions. Habits can be difficult to break, due to the deeply rooted neural pathways that allow us to operate on autopilot, but they are not impossible and usually not dangerous to break on our own.

For example, if I want to break the habit of chewing my fingernails, I might apply a bad tasting substance to my nails to jar me from the automatic behavior of putting my fingernail in my mouth to bite it. While this would be inconvenient and uncomfortable for me, ridding myself of my nail-biting habit probably isn't going to greatly destabilize my psychological health.

Addiction, on the other hand, is a habitual dependence on something. No matter how hard you try, you can't stop, and when you try to stop you experience a destabilization of your physical and mental state of being. Over time, drug use results in a dependency that makes it increasingly difficult stop using the drugs.

Perhaps you began an addictive behavior because you received positive reinforcement for doing it. For example, the pleasure of the high inspired you to want to get high again and again, or the approval of your peers made you feel on top of the world.

Often, especially with substance abuse, what begins with positive reinforcement can quickly transition into negative reinforcement. What started out as a fun high or a laugh in the city park with your buddies is now an addiction because you don't want to deal with the pain of withdrawal if you stop using the substance. It's less painful, overall, to keep using it than it is to stop.

Of course, there are happy stories out there of people who quit their addictions through pure willpower, but they are more rare than you might believe. Addictions are unhealthy physiological needs. When you stop the addictive behavior, your body goes through withdrawals, in which you experience physical, mental, and emotional symptoms.

You may have learned to function in normal manner with the addictive behavior in place, and when you remove that, you find that you can no longer function in daily life. People will notice that you don't have it together, and they will see and judge your problems. This is a huge obstacle. Admitting to yourself that you have an addiction is hard enough, but when quitting means that you might have to sacrifice your pride in front of all the people in your life you've felt that you must perform for, that's a whole new can of worms.

CBT Techniques for Overcoming Addiction

While I highly recommend that you obtain professional help with your addiction as well, the following are some CBT techniques that are designed to help you target the root causes of your addiction and give you some tools for resisting the addictive behavior.

Identify Your Reasons

So you want to quit your addiction. It's time to make two lists. The first is a benefits list. What are the benefits of continuing with your addiction? These might include any of the above reasons or plenty of other possibilities. The purpose of the benefits list is to find out what events and emotions led to your addiction. As previously stated, many addictions stem from other problems that you didn't know how to deal with at the time. Identifying these roots will allow you to revisit them and come up with healthy ways to learn how to cope. This can be hard. Opening up about painful emotions or traumatic events is never easy, but it will make long term recovery more manageable if you can eliminate these reasons for needing drugs from your benefits list.

Because recovery from addiction can be such a long, arduous process, also identify your reasons for wanting to quit you addiction. Is it negatively impacting the people you love the most? Is it affecting your ability to support yourself or maintain your job or career? Has it taken away your hobbies by consuming all of your free time? Has it put you thousands of dollars in debt? Has it taken away your health? Corroded your friendships? Made you hate yourself?

All of these are motivations for quitting. Keep them close for when you're tempted to throw in the towel.

Find A Healthy Replacement

If the reason for your addiction stems from not knowing how to deal with stress, come up with a healthier way to deal with your stress. These might include exercising, meditating, calm breathing, talking with a friend, or any positive activity that reminds you that you are stronger than your addiction, and you can do this.

Replacement activities are a great, tangible way to start, but you shouldn't ignore your own thought patterns. It's probable that you've fallen into a negative way of thinking about yourself that reinforces your addictive behavior.

Do you easily beat yourself up over small and large failures alike? Are you quick to jump to the conclusion that you are an addict because you are incompetent, undeserving, stupid, lazy, or worthless?

These ideas make up the negative self-talk that helps perpetuate your problem. Identify those times when you are most likely to tell yourself these things and then ask yourself for evidence. What is your evidence that you are lazy or worthless, and is that a fair conclusion to jump to? Perhaps it would be more accurate to say that your addiction makes you feel out of control. Your addiction makes you *feel* like you don't deserve a happy life.

Acknowledge how you *feel*, but instead of turning those into "I am" statements, turn them into "I feel" statements. Saying, "I am," has an air of finality that can make the negative statement more difficult to overcome. Instead of telling yourself, "I am an addict," it can be more helpful to say, "I have an addiction." You are not your addiction.

Correcting the way you think about yourself and your emotions in relation to your addiction can go a long way toward helping you recover from it.

Develop a Strategy

Every person is different, and the strategy that might work exceedingly well for one person, might be a total flop for another person. You need to come up with your own personalized plan for eliminating your addictive behaviors and coping with your feelings and emotions. The type of addiction you have might tend toward different treatment methodologies.

For example, for heavy drug use, the best strategy might be to check yourself into a hospital, where doctors can monitor you while you detox and go through the most painful part of the withdrawals. It might then be wise to find a halfway house or someplace where you can get away from the triggers of your normal environment. In the early stages of addiction recovery you are often the most fragile, because you haven't yet learned the techniques you need to cope with your regular life.

Join a supportive community. Maybe this is a local chapter of AA. Maybe it's a group of friends and family members who love you and want to help you overcome your addiction. It's harder to stop trying when you have people cheering for you every step of the way and asking you how you're doing.

Especially in the early stages of recovery, avoiding those high-risk situations altogether might be best. If gambling is your addiction, don't go to the casino. If you're addicted to alcohol, it's a good idea to avoid parties where there will be alcohol, remove all alcoholic substances from your home, and stay away from bars, clubs, or restaurants that serve alcohol.

Likewise, it's a good idea to avoid people who typically encourage you to participate in high-risk situations. Sometimes, especially in cases of drug and alcohol abuse, it's best to move to a new town to get a clean start and get away from the things and people who influenced you to use.

You probably won't be able to avoid high risk situations for forever, and for some addictions, like over-eating, it's impossible to really get away from the opportunity to engage in addictive behaviors, so you'll need to practice techniques for coping with stress and temptation.

Explore the positive and negative consequences of engaging in the addictive behavior: what will happen if I drink too much tonight? What will happen if I say no? What will happen if I eat more than a healthy serving of dinner tonight? How will I feel if I only eat the serving in front of me? Saying no to addiction is hard, but each time you say it, you should feel proud of yourself. Let each no you say bolster your confidence.

Learn to self-monitor in order to recognize your cravings early: notice what emotions and behaviors make you want to indulge in the addictive behavior. What feelings lead to you need a cigarette? Do you tend to overeat in conjunction with watching a lot of TV? Is it hardest to say no to drinking when you're alone in the evenings and your family members are away doing their evening activities?

Is there something else you can do to re-allocate the addiction? For example, you might thwart the addiction by chewing gum when you crave a cigarette or going for a run when you start to feel like binge drinking. If aloneness and loneliness tend to trigger your cravings, maybe you can find a friend to move in with you or set up evening plans with friends for yourself so that you don't spend entire evenings by yourself.

Perhaps you don't have close friends anymore, because your addiction has pushed them away. You're never too old to make friends. If you like to knit, you might check your area online for a knitting group. If you're spiritual or want to get back into your religion, join a church or temple. Take a group class. Join a community service project. Once you start looking, you'll probably find a hundred healthy things you can do with your free time that get you out of your own mind and out with people.

Of course, it takes time form deep relationships with new people, but taking initiative helps. If you meet someone you'd like to know better, ask them to coffee. Get to know them. Open up to them about yourself and your daily struggles to stay clean from your addiction.

Being open about yourself and your problems is really hard, but it can also be very freeing and enlightening. Of course there will be some people out there who will judge you, but a lot of people will be very happy for your decision to improve yourself and do what they can to be supportive.

At the end of the day, no matter what your cravings are or what your traitorous self-talk is trying to say, you are not alone. You are worthy of creating a better life for yourself. You can do this.

CHAPTER FIVE: OVERCOMING DEPRESSION

Depression is probably one of the most misunderstood mental illnesses of our society. Coupled with the fact that so many people have experienced it, this is unsettling. How many people with depression have been told that all they have to do is pull themselves up by the bootstraps and move forward? Would you tell a person with cancer stop all the chemotherapy and just target positive thoughts at the cancerous part of your body? That would be ridiculous.

Some people use the word depression interchangeably with sadness or boredom. For these people, pulling themselves up by the bootstraps is an option. For people suffering from chronic depression, if we could simply pull on our bootstraps and click our heels to feel happy, we would do it in a heartbeat. Many of us have tried.

It's easy to confuse depression with chronic pessimism and assume that if the person would just get over himself and stop dwelling on all of the negative stuff, he could be happy like anyone else. For a chronic Debbie Downer, this is certainly the answer, but for a person with chronic depression, the problem is often much deeper than a matter of willpower and a large dose of optimism.

What is depression? It's a loss of motivation and interest in participating in activities that were formerly of interest. It's an inability or reduced ability to participate in and enjoy life. It's a decreased ability to function within social groups or work settings. It's a feeling of sadness or of being down that is often paired with a loss of appetite, inability to sleep well, feelings of guilt, and thoughts about death or suicide. Sometimes depression can arise from environmental causes, and sometimes it's the result of a chemical imbalance within the brain.

I spent several months beating myself up over the fact that no matter how hard I tried, I couldn't seem to beat my depression with CBT. Lucy finally persuaded me to see a doctor about it, and I was put on a mood stabilizer. Paired with CBT, this was a winning combination. I still had depressive episodes, but I was able to get through them and see a light at the end of the tunnel.

Even better, once I was able to remove myself from the toxic environment of my mother's house, and find a place of my own, I found that my depressive episodes decreased in frequency and duration dramatically. I visited the doctor once again, and he theorized that it might be safe to wean me off of the medication. At that point, I found that I was able to handle myself with the CBT techniques without help from the medication.

That is not to say that I never feel depressed; I still do sometimes, but I am able to manage my depression such that I no longer get caught up for very long in the self-fulfilling prophecies of negative self-thought.

Steps and Techniques for Overcoming Depression With CBT

The following is a list of steps and techniques to help you overcome your depression.

Practice Noticing

Practice noticing your thoughts, feelings, and behaviors in any given situation. Don't judge yourself, and, when you're starting out, don't immediately attempt to analyze yourself. Your only task to take note of how your depression makes you feel physically and emotionally and then note what you do when you feel that way.

Do you shut off your alarm, pull the quilt over your face, and sleep for the rest of the day? Do you eat more or less than usual? Are you uninterested in activities you usually enjoy? Do you gain or lose weight? Do sleep more or less?

Also notice what you tell yourself when you experience depression. Do you tell yourself that you're lazy or impotent? Do you beat yourself up for not feeling like doing anything?

Is there something in particular that tends to trigger depressive episodes? Do you usually experience depression after you visit your mentally ill mother? Is it when your spouse criticizes you? Is it when you fail a test or bomb a work presentation? Or does it seem to come on at random?

This first phase is simply for collecting data. The more you notice about yourself, the better grasp you will have on your depression in later steps.

Pick a Change

Depression is a vicious cycle. The more you think it and feel it, the more you behave in a depressed manner. Since many of the behaviors of depression are fertile ground for thoughts and feelings to run unchecked through your brain, they tend to more firmly plan the thoughts in your head. Behaviors and thoughts thus reinforce each other.

To break the vicious cycle, you need to change either a thought or a behavior. When it comes to depression, it's sometimes easier to change a behavior. Instead of pulling your covers back over your head, make yourself get up and face the day. You won't magically feel not depressed, but forcing yourself to do something serves the dual purpose of attempting to break the downward thought spiral that takes place when you spend the day avoiding it and ruminating over your depression and forcing your to focus your mind, at least for short, temporary spurts, on something different.

Enlist the help of a friend to take away your blankets, throw your clothes at you, and make you eat some breakfast. There's a popular saying, "Fake it till you make it." Don't pretend like you're not depressed—that will be unsuccessful, and it's unrealistic—but don't let your depression have the final say. Whether you feel like doing anything with your life today or not, get up and find one thing, however small, to accomplish. Maybe that's mowing the lawn. Heck, maybe it's just putting on pants. Take any victory you can.

Pleasant Activity Scheduling

In the throes of depression, it's common to lose interest in activities that you normally enjoy. You don't feel like doing anything, and you feel that doing even formerly enjoyable activities won't help you, so you don't do anything. It's a loop that is bound to bring you deeper into your depression.

Instead, schedule activities and stick to the schedule. You probably won't feel better right away, but you will have at least be able to stop the downward spiral that not doing anything will push you down. This technique is usually the most effective when your plans involve others, who can help hold you to them and also distract you from your destructive internal monologue. Visit a friend, go bowling, go out on the town, have a game night, go to a movie.

Analyze and Adapt

Identify situations that lead you to feel depressed or more depressed than usual. Maybe that's hanging out with overly negative friends. Maybe it's trying to deal with an impossible family situation. Maybe it's a verbally abusive spouse. Maybe it's a competitive coworker who's trying to get you fired.

If it's possible, try to avoid some of these situations while you learn to get a grasp on your first CBT techniques. Of course, you can't spend your life avoiding hard stuff just to feel happy. You can't skip work or ignore your significant other. That's not how the world works, but while you're trying to get a grip on your negative and harmful thought patterns, it can be helpful to remove some of the variables and obstacles. Maybe you have a friend who is constantly criticizing your life choices. Maybe you need to see her less or not at all for a while.

Next, you need to identify any thoughts or patterns that tend to lead to depressive episodes or keep you trapped within them. These can include thoughts like, "Why even try, because I'll never succeed," "I'm a worthless lump who can't do anything right," or "I'm a lazy, miserable person." These are assumptions you are making about yourself and your worth that aren't true. Repeating them often to yourself or letting your mind run wild with them is creating a self-fulfilling prophecy. As I have repeatedly said, you become what you practice. Practice negative self-talk, and you will train yourself to be negative.

When you find the negative thoughts that tend to lead you more rapidly into a depressive state, practice replacing these thoughts with positive thoughts about yourself. Write them down. "I like that I'm an empathetic person." "I'm good at identifying strengths in others." "My friends love me." "I am worthy of respect and attention." "I am a fun, engaging person who just happens to feel down right now." It feels stupid, especially at first, but look yourself in the eye while standing in front of your mirror, and say your positive self-thoughts out loud. Repeat this exercise a couple of times every day, and you will train your mind to have positive automatic thoughts about yourself with more frequency.

Will these CBT techniques completely cure your depression? They might, but they don't always. They haven't for me. I still feel prone to depression sometimes. The difference is that now I have the tools I need to bring myself out of my slump. I understand that I can acknowledge my feelings without dwelling for too long on them, and I can usually find a suitable distraction for myself, like going out with a friend or watching a movie, that can halt the depressive episode before it has a chance to spiral out of control.

CHAPTER SIX: OVERCOMING ANXIETIES

We all experience anxiety. It's a normal life emotion that is manageable for most people when it occurs—a stressful work situation, an important exam, a relationship tension. At healthy, manageable levels, anxiety, much like fear, can even be a great motivator toward accomplishing goals and signifying how much you care about something or someone. While the techniques to follow in this chapter can, or course, be useful for coping with normal anxiety, they are especially geared toward coping with the other kind.

Anxiety becomes a problem that must be overcome when it is experienced at such extreme levels that it interferes with one's ability to lead a healthy, fulfilling life. If you experience feelings of panic or unease, heart palpitations, insomnia, muscle tension, dizziness, nausea, tingling or numbness in the hands or feet, or shortness of breath, then you may be experiencing symptoms extreme anxiety.

Anxiety manifests itself in a lot of different ways: panic disorders, social anxiety disorders, specific phobias, and generalized anxiety disorders. If you have one of these disorders, it's not your fault or the result of a character flaw, and it's possible to learn to overcome the anxiety. Some people are prone to anxiety, and this will require a lifestyle change.

CBT is almost always the best method that is currently available for treating anxiety and anxiety-related disorders. While medications can treat the symptoms of anxiety, CBT seeks to find the root of the problem and educate you on how to cope with anxiety in the healthiest manner possible. The goal of CBT isn't to eliminate your anxiety but to give you techniques to push through it and not let it control your life.

CBT is often more effective than medications because it gives you a permanent solution to a lifelong problem rather than a bandage fix and a dependency on anti-psychotics or anti-depressants.

Keep in mind that while a lot of cases of anxiety disorders are effectively treated without medication, it's not a character defect if you try CBT and still need medication in order to help you regulate your anxiety. This is something you should talk with your doctor about.

CBT is usually the most effective form of therapy used to treat anxiety. Unlike purely using exposure therapy, which is associated with the gross stereotype of curing anxiety about germs by swimming in manure and any number of unsanitary things, CBT focuses on the interaction between thoughts and behaviors and works on consciously reformatting subconscious thought patterns. No crap needed.

CBT teaches you how to recognize negative cognitive distortions, challenge them, and replace them with positive thoughts. You might get anxious about going to parties because you fear you will throw up and people will think you are crazy. Here, the cognitive distortion is that you are jumping to conclusions and assuming that if you throw up at a party, people will think you're crazy. You might instead tell yourself that people are more likely to think that you're sick and make sure that you're okay.

When it comes to anxiety, CBT is what helps you reframe your thoughts and beliefs. If you worry that you might contract germs and diseases and then die you might tell yourself that you worry that you're a dirty person who might contract bad germs and die. CBT teaches you to notice the inaccuracy in this statement—that you are a dirty person. You are a clean person who worries about being contaminated with germs. Your problem isn't your filth but your debilitating worry.

Some disorders, like Obsessive-Compulsive Disorder, are like bullies—the more you give in to their demands, the more they will demand of you. For example, if you give in to washing your hands three times, you will more easily give in to washing them five or ten times later on. OCD itself isn't about danger; it's about worry about danger. The worry becomes so prominent that you can't escape it, and that's when it becomes unhealthy. That's how it is with a lot of anxiety disorders.

A person with an anxiety disorder might tend to always react as the though the predicted negative outcome is going to happen, even if it's not probable. Realizing that you have an option in your thoughts can help to break the anxiety cycle and help you manage and overcome the anxious feelings in order to live out a healthy, fulfilling life. CBT helps you reframe your self-thought so that you are able to view things in a more positive light.

Managing Anxiety With CBT

CBT has been proven over and over again to be one of the most effective methods for dealing with anxiety and diminishing its effects.

The following are some CBT techniques that can be used one at a time or simultaneously with other techniques.

Calm Breathing

The first, most basic relaxation technique you can practice is Calm Breathing. In calm breathing, breaths should come slowly and from deep inside of you, from your abdomen or diaphragm rather than from your chest. Take about four seconds to inhale slowly through your nose. Hold the breath for one or two seconds, and then slowly release the breath through your mouth. Pause for a couple of seconds before beginning your next breath. Repeat this cycle six to eight times.

This rhythm is designed to regulate your oxygen intake and prevent over breathing, which can lead to hyperventilating. Hyperventilating and over breathing have been repeatedly proven to add to anxiety. Calm breathing battles this.

Calm breathing won't take away your anxiety, but it can take the edge off and help you endure the anxious feelings.

For the best results, practice calm breathing for five minutes every day, even if you don't feel anxious. Calm breathing is a skill, and practicing this technique when you're already calm will help you be able to more easily access it when you are anxious.

If you want to play a Mozart concerto in concert for an audience, then you have to practice when you are alone so that your fingers have mastered the movements and you are able to perform under stress. Calm breathing works in the same way. Practice it when you are calm, and you'll be able to perform it much more easily when you're anxious.

Progressive Muscle Relaxation

Another relaxation technique is called Progressive Muscle Relaxation. When you're dealing with anxiety, it's common to have tense muscles all day long without realizing it. This activity helps you learn how to differentiate between a tense muscle and a relaxed muscle through a process of tensing and releasing certain muscle groups.

To get started, put on loose clothing and find a comfortable place, like a reclining chair, where you will be undisturbed for fifteen minutes. Take five calm breaths.

Next, you will isolate and tense different muscle groups for five seconds while you inhale slowly. For example, you might start with your foot and tense it by curling your toes down. Hold this for five seconds, taking care to only tense the muscles in the isolated area. When five seconds are up, exhale while you let the tension flow out of the isolated muscles. The point of this activity is to learn how to differentiate between tense and relaxed muscles, so pay special attention to how your muscles feel when they are completely tensed as opposed to completely relaxed.

Take care not to hurt yourself while tensing your muscles. Shaking from the tension is normal, but shooting pain is not.

The target muscle groups include: the foot, the lower leg and foot, and the entire hand; the hand and then the entire arm; the buttocks; the stomach; the chest; the neck and shoulders; the mouth; the eyes; and the forehead. You should do your right and left arms and legs separately.

This activity can be easier when you have a voice taking you through each of the steps. Many relaxation CDs are available online if you'd like to explore that option, or you might have a friend walk you through the steps, reminding you to inhale with the tension and exhale as you let it go for each step.

When you've become acquainted with the muscles of your body and their tensions, this technique can be shortened into just four muscle groups: your lower body; your core; your arms, shoulders, and neck; and your face.

Once you're a pro at being able to tell if your muscles are relaxes or tense, you can move on to the release only technique. To do this, you simply identify which muscles in your body are currently tense, and you release them. It sounds easy, but it takes a lot of practice to be able to pinpoint where your body is tense, so don't be discouraged if it takes several sessions of tensing and releasing isolated muscle groups before you are able to accomplish this.

Like with calm breathing, practicing progressive muscle relaxation when you're calm will help you utilize it when you're anxious. Also, like with calm breathing, muscle relaxation won't fix your anxiety, but it should help you steady yourself to ride through your emotions more gracefully.

Realistic Thinking

Realistic thinking is a huge part of CBT. With anxiety, the key is to avoid having or creating thoughts that are overly negative or overly positive. When you have a negative thought, you don't have to sugarcoat it for yourself by denying your anxiety or telling yourself that you have no reason to be anxious. Instead, be balanced. Instead of saying, "I'm too anxious. I can't do this," tell yourself, "It's okay that I feel anxious, but I won't let it stop me from going through with my social plans."

Remember that it's okay to feel anxious. Feelings of anxiety aren't dangerous or bad in and of themselves, and giving yourself permission to acknowledge that they are real is important. For example, when a loved one dies, feeling sad is a legitimate response. When you're about to give a huge presentation, feeling nervous or anxious is legitimate.

Note when your emotions shift and ask yourself what you are telling yourself right now and what specific thought is upsetting you. Examine whether you are falling into a negative thought trap. Are you telling yourself that a friend canceling your plans at the last second means you must be worthless? What is your evidence for jumping to this conclusion? Is your friend canceling because she hates you, or is it because she had a stressful situation come up at work? Are you confusing a possibility with a probability? After all, just because something is possible, doesn't make it probable. Don't borrow trouble.

The final step in realistic thinking is to replace negative thoughts with more balanced views. You might tell yourself, "I have dealt with situations like this before, and I know how to do it again," and, "I am brave for confronting what makes me anxious." Your anxious feelings are legitimate, but don't give them so much importance that they control how or if you have relationships and whether you are able to live your life in the best way possible.

Exposure

The best short-term solution to dealing with anxiety is to avoid situations that make you anxious. Sometimes this is the best call, but if you want to achieve long-term mastery over your anxiety, it is imperative that you learn to face stressful situations.

The first step in exposure is to make a list of situations or objects that make you anxious. Rate them on a scale of one to ten for how anxious each one makes you feel. You might rate going to the grocery store as a two, making small talk with coworkers as a four, and confronting your boss about workplace conflicts that are minimizing productivity as a ten. Write down as many situations as you can think of.

The next step is to choose whatever you rated as the least anxiety-inducing and expose yourself to that situation repeatedly until you start to feel less anxious when you encounter it. When you have reduced your anxiety by half for the first thing on your list, move up to the next item and repeat the cycle until you have cut your anxiety for this situation or activity in half.

The more you practice exposing yourself to stressful situations the more used to them you will become.

You don't need to go into these situations unequipped, however. If you've been practicing calm breathing, bring that technique with you into exposure and use it to help keep your breathing regulated. The same goes for muscle relaxation and realistic thinking. Whatever techniques you have practiced outside of anxious situations will be yours to call on during exposure.

Preventing an Anxiety Relapse

A relapse is a total return to your old behaviors and thoughts. It is what happens when you lose all of the improvements you made before you had the chance to ingrain your new behaviors and thoughts as habits. It's sort of like exercising in that way. You have to practice regularly in order to get stronger, and if you stop practicing, then your muscles will atrophy and return to their former state.

Here are some tips to prevent relapsing.

Keep Practicing!

Practicing your anxiety management techniques is the most important thing you can do to prevent a relapse. It's like studying for a pop quiz; you might not know when the quiz is going to occur, but it you've been studying daily for it, then you'll be prepared for whatever hits you.

Anxiety is similar. Practice dealing with your small daily anxieties, and when overly stressful situations occur, you will be able to weather them without relapsing. When training for a marathon, you don't have to practice the whole marathon in order to finish on race day. Daily shorter runs will benefit you more than sporadic long longs. Your most anxious situations will be overcome through practice with smaller anxieties.

Challenge Yourself

Just because you've learned a couple of techniques that work for dealing with your anxiety doesn't mean that you should stop learning new ones. There's always a chance that you will find something that works more effectively for dealing with your anxiety or that some new area of research is being opened up. Continually learning and growing will give you more tools in your kit to combat potential relapses.

Know Your Red Flags

Make a list of warning signs that signify an episode of anxiety and situations that might cause it so that you can consciously identify if you are entering into a tough situation. This way, you can implement your coping techniques before your anxiety has an opportunity to get out of control and start controlling you.

Warning signs might include combativeness with loved ones, increased heart rate in anxious situations, and thoughts that are anxious and negative. When you notice these, it's time to implement the techniques you've practiced.

Be Kind To Yourself

Remember that a lapse is not a relapse. Losing control one time does not mean that you're a failure or that you've undone all of your hard work. In fact, CBT can be described as riding a bike. Even if you've been riding for a while, you might still fall off of it, but that doesn't mean that you no longer know how to ride a bike. Once you've learned the CBT techniques, no one can take them away from you, and the more you practice them, the less likely you are to stumble or lapse during difficult situations.

Also remember that lapses are bound to happen at some point. Lapses aren't failures, and you should not let them lead you to believe that you failed or that you're an idiot. This kind of negative thought will only propel you downward into your old anxious thought patterns.

Try to understand why a particular situation caused you to lapse and come up with a plan to cope better the next time. Then, forgive yourself.

CONCLUSION: A BENEDICTION

Sometimes I still retreat to my imaginary chateau and gaze out over the placid waters and imagine the sweet, cool breeze on my face. The difference now is that I do so in moments of calm, when I feel happy.

Since I've moved away from my mom's house, I've found less and less need for the imaginary retreat. My new job is satisfactory, my apartment is tranquil and decorated in bright colors and soft furniture, and the friends I have made since opening myself up to others are amazing and supportive.

My prayer is that I've said something in this book about CBT that can help you improve your life in some small way. I don't have all the answers, but I have a few of them, and I thank you for the opportunity to let me share a piece of my story. I hope that adding my story to the fabric of your life will bring you that much closer to conquering the world.

Bibliography

E. Heidari, A. Banerjee, J. T. Newton. Oral
    health status of non-phobic and dentally
    phobic individuals; a secondary analysis
    of the 2009 Adult Dental Health Survey.
    BDJ, 2015; 219 (9): E9 DOI:
    10.1038/sj.bdj.2015.853

Helms, L. (2013). Cognitive Behavioral Tools.
    Retrieved April 12, 2016, from
    https://www.youtube.com/watch?v=IEsY
    iCDoJks

King's College London. (2015, November 27).
    Cognitive behavior therapy can help
    overcome fear of the dentist.
    ScienceDaily. Retrieved April 12, 2016
    from
    www.sciencedaily.com/releases/2015/11/
    151127102335.htm\

Myers, D. G. (2011). *Exploring psychology*. New
    York, NY: Worth.

Segell, M. (1998). Big mystery: What causes addiction? Retrieved April 12, 2016, from http://www.nbcnews.com/id/3076712/t/ big-mystery-what-causes-addiction/#.VwyEK3CARJM

Self Help - Cognitive-Behavioural Therapy (CBT). (2010). Retrieved April 12, 2016, from http://www.anxietybc.com/help-resources/cbt/self-help-cognitive-behavioural-therapy

Smith, M., & Segall, J. (2016). Overcoming Drug Addiction. Retrieved April 12, 2016, from http://www.helpguide.org/articles/addict ion/overcoming-drug-addiction.htm

Trauma. (n.d.). Retrieved April 12, 2016, from http://www.apa.org/topics/trauma/